GW00801785

Also by Annie Katchinska

Faber New Poets 6 (Faber & Faber, 2010)

Natto (If a Leaf Falls, 2018)

AURORA TOWN

Katchinska

ISBN: 978-1-913642-75-4

Cover design by Aaron Kent

Edited & typeset by Aaron Kent

Broken Sleep Books (2021)

Broken Sleep Books Ltd
Rhydwen,
Talgarreg,
SA44 4HB
Wales

Contents

Aurora Town

Annie Katchinska

Music of another church

Alleluia – a story of want –
Alleluia, in root beer tongues
He is a good warrior in his tight jacket
Alleluia, felt tip, Alleluia, God-wristband
Aquarium lights say to me, Alleluia
Anthems say, Alleluia
And snow like heaps of polar bears in all directions, Alleluia
Alleluia, wherever you are – you're with the BBC
Consequently no longer foreigners, strangers
Alleluia, cute friend, let us pray for your headache
Alleluia lay our hands Alleluia Alleluia
She's an angel with a microphone, Alleluia
My heart to be scrubbed, Alleluia
Alleluia, fall on your knees
Alleluia, blister of a Sunday
Altar call –
Tick off your sins –
And this girl with no gift but you, Alleluia, no skin
Until I touched you, no words until I spoke you,
I offer my tortoiseshell eyes for you to peel off,
I didn't know water until I was up
And it splashed around me like nothing, a promise
To never go back
Alleluia, never
Forget – but now –
Our bodies stumpy sticks of chalk
Flamingo Motel, Alleluia
Intentional, Alleluia
Our guilty worshipful Alleluia
Our worshipful skins
And a long bright list of what you are not
And my body crumbly with shame, Alleluia
Apocrypha, Alleluia
Again they would say Rejoice Rejoice
No shortage of butter here in milk heaven
Don't wrestle from the bunch, little grapes
But Alleluia, wrestle – twist –
Alleluia, Dead Sea
Alleluia, taste it
O taste and gargle and spit

Here I am

When the ticking month was over
did she get on a plane, fly over two continents
and land in a bristling city,
I mean did she walk
onto and off of a plane
and stumble
into a gangly hotel
and had she signed up for this to see
what would happen and now it was happening
and when she woke up
in a shaking hotel did it rock her
like a shining mother
and was there on the bedside table
this half-eaten dinner, this jumbo rice ball,
and what did she do next,
how will she tell it?

At the ticking end of the month
did Sapporo arch its back, unfurl a paw
to snatch her up as she stepped off the plane,
I mean did her feet walk her
into and out of that useful sky
and stumble her
into a gangly but strong hotel
and was this happening
now because she signed up
and when the movement woke her
was she a child inside a mother
as tall and swaying as a hotel
and on the side her headphones, the song
where maybe he gets on a plane, and though
what happened next was years ago,
will she tell it?

1.

Susukino

i.
Our first time downtown
we were not two weeks off the plane

and thinner, cleaner, *too young for this mess*
he diagnosed and touched my arm unasked so now let's go

here I am with my seasonal tricks,
nails and hips and anklebones

and a taste in my hair and gin in my shoes
needing week after week to go where everyone goes

ii.
With garblemouth I try to explain.
With a mouthful of sand I turn to this boy,
with a mouth tuna-swollen, beer-mucked
I try to explain
but we're on the long trek down to the next place
With a chapped small mouth
With a mouth like With a mouth like
With a mouth fish-hooked
Here, he says
and we're this gaggle,
ten-foot
bottles pour
Sprite
on girls in
Cheburashka
furs
who can't
believe
their luck as we float
towards them, such balloons   *wait*
stop
a bathroom,
my purpling mouth,
watch me step out
bump against this spike
and click and crack till the *right song* flicks

and they come to me, talk to me, hear me, adore me,
recoil at my lip blood,
salt.

iii.

You found us on the twentieth floor   and we think we have nothing to do
with you   who found us soaked   juices   stomachs   you pull her by
her snapped tooth onto the table   and say dance dance   you the syrupy
lizard of grammar and error   she saw you in the airport   in the Tokyo hotel
coathangers trembling   she is ripped roots   she is not quite   she can't
remember how this makes her feel like   how does it go   she can't help it
is she blending in okay   has she found the new culture   is it in this tight
dripping booth and is she   loving it enough   is she still a fun gaijingirl or
is that just   you take your time with us   lick the spilt drink from our necks
pluck our accents away   we all talk   like this   like this   there are so
many things we want   but not this   you   take   your   time   I look
up, try to reach for a window

iv.

if we wait an hr the subway'll creep back to life
but ASAHI   KIRIN   NIKKA

                                        already look sick,
their letters blink, judder
so hunger
          leads to this plasticky bread,
          pink meat and no wait what even is this
what is this   illiterate clattering
in a ketchup-coloured fast food pitstop
there for women to slump

                              over tables and sleep
          till it's done
                    or rub sauce on their skirts,
or simply
sit and *cry* and *text*
                    and you and I are not friends yet,
                    we just washed up on the shore

          at the same time roughly

                                        now let me
                                        curl up
                                        metallic and cold
          lemon-sticky
                         greased shut

14

v.
Got to get on it got to shake jetlag
          What time is it? What time should I be?
Fruitpeel and fridgewhir and neighbourclunk only –
          Just perched on this random bit of the earth

Come to me   come now
I'm chopped up thick   I live like
raw squid   expectant

Pods

& we holler & clap even though we're uncertain
but the all-you-can-drink-&-roar deal is 7hrs long
& we know at least that once we start it'll stream
those clips of breezy baywatched America, so we
click on the mic & sing for a tram in springtime
San Francisco, sing for a bar in Texas, stand on
chairs for *Once more you open the door* & we're
a blonde girl leaning her elbows on a fence or a
blonde girl at the mirror looking past the camera,
we *turn around! – bright! – eyes!* for local history
museums & Boston, the great wash of New Jersey
& fuzzy California, a West Coast state smooth as
an apple pip so let's dial for a pitcher, can you get
us another Moscow Mule, can you gimme the mic,
can you pass me my bag, we know you're the only
one who says it properly, *ka-ra-oh-keh*, but don't
be a prick, & a clock tower, a bouquet, a girl in the
distance, girl in a dark plaid shirt with a milkshake,
so what good would living do me when we're a
roomful of slobbering songbirds maybe homesick
for beach towns, or Portland, or maybe not, our
Wuthering Wuthering Wuthering Heights thrown
up to the top floor where the booths are smaller,
they're really just pods & each pod (so the legend
goes) contains one wiry singer with loosened
necktie & a half-spilt Asahi, & who among us now
wants to wake up, who would want that saliva?

Oden

Tofu, egg: familiar
shapes in the broth
Other stodgy fairies
bob alongside Can't
name the liquid
itself, or the stink
Full moon radish
sliced Boiled clear
Jostling dumpling,
mushroom, fish
sausage, quivering
fishy fish-jelly
It comes down to
this winter staple
they urge me
Down to this
mottled, flecked
snow Shocking
alien pressed
to glass My days
all glass to moth
against Smack
and rub and never
get right Not
knowing what's
true Fear of first
snow A simmering
winter A hotpot
of creatures,
flickers, crops
to try to love
To chew

Natto

it comes down to this string
stuff, tang of mustard and soy
so quick, first time to realise
the gloop of a life, lifting and
balancing tricksy beans like
babies, fat and chewy babies
to swallow, fingers scrape
a paper pot, salty mistrust
curled in the futon as hours
ferment, humiliate, ambition
gone stringy with no hope
ever of ropes, clues, tearful
soybean falls uphill uphill
and what it comes down to

Negative Pocket

HERE WE GO the woman says opening the door to the insect circus

this is where beetles tremble in ice

wind up the tightropes

sorry for disturbing

all weekend I don't actually speak

I stack tin cans in an earthquake kit

a bluebottle towers by the trapdoor

five hundred yen for the beak of a crow

the boy who was screamed at this morning

drinks carton after carton of milk

until his classmates forgive him

kanji fall down the chalkboard like snow

in a corner marked CROWS there's a glow worm in a box

hot eggy cabbagey pancake

potato curry baguette

glittery fleas stuck round a mirror where you can see my shins

a dirty flying ant

battling my breath's

clumsy cartwheels

it comes down

the snow comes very sorry

I stagger to the trapdoor's delicate sign

PLEASE TOUCH THE BLUEBOTTLE GENTLY

Snow Festival

What kuma really wants to do is start the year again and again until it's right
but everyone at the local shrine has a fortune in one hand, a hot dog in the other.
kuma arrived in summer, sniffed the work visa, signed the contract KUMA, and now

this bear cub's alone and trying in a city that's cold beyond all warning, and
kuma's feet gnaw and twist, and kuma's love isn't here. This is how the country:
this is how the country begins to slither: kuma gulps unfamiliar dinners, gains this

thick predictable weight, in the slushy bus station the small man is grinning and naked
under his wax coat, and when kuma falls out of the taxi kuma throws up in the snow,
three sloppy peanut splats to bury in more snow: and this is how the country: this is

how: on every megastore's top floor the popstars glow, tilt heads and hips, they're
cupcakes, strawberries, angels smeared and stretched: this is how the country
kuma cannot love begins to slither around kuma like chicken skin greasy and wrong,

sling it off, wherever you go there you sputter, cold thumbs, a fall on the ice. But it's
festival season kuma, kuma, a city of sculpted white animals and chiselled sparkly
ice cartoons, Australian tourists slip and slide, mushroom soup from Aibetsu that

tastes like mushroom soup, *let's go see the snow sculptures/how do I eat this crab.*
Enormous snow tajmahal snow mickeymouse snowrocket, and in underground walkways
a stout pickled kuma, kuma's been picked up and dropped in this postcard *why did you*

20

come here how long will you stay but here is kuma despite despite – Fight against the sweep of it, kuma can't – Disentangle what kuma wants from what kuma wants to want – Rice dumplings settle heavy in kuma's stomach like snow. kuma never knew. Early sun

makes the snow blue and yellow, train carriages rattle with snowboarding gear but kuma gets there and the surgery's closed, kuma's baby language buckles, *Hello my name is nice to meet you please be good to me* a big and wobbly kuma face, long and soupy kuma arms,

kuma is a desperate kuma encased in ice. kuma knows it's never home. There are bears on the city's outskirts, not button-faced, no porridge paws or fur like sugary buckwheat but a rough invasion the city will not assimilate. Down blizzardy Route 36 lined with

snowheaps the nurses are baffled at fat foreign kuma, how pale kuma is, how kuma squanders, how a barren kuma, how kuma is orthopaedic hospital and fear of pain needing some some some kind of salvation, needing to split split – split – split open –

The girls arrive

No other Sunday for the girls except –

they are cankerous, they smell of stale rice, their cardigans are buttoned wrong, they hesitate to enter the room but look, the eyes that meet their eyes are sugar, sugar-water – and the girls have come for something to cherish, their wants as round and flat as plates, they're only here to see, to check, they wouldn't normally no *never never* if it weren't for this, mealy shuddering unable to stand it, the girls tumble in so certain that music is harmless and they are not stupid girls tomorrow or Tuesday they can stop anytime, only squares of tissue paper, only tissue women on spilt cherry juice.

The girls listen, exhausted – The girls are welcomed – The girls will prosper – The girls are such fruit – The girls have their true names squeaked in felt tip – The girls will stand under the shower later with *kingdom kingdom kingdom* gushing from the tub, flooding the floor, billowing up in devoted clouds but for now here they are the good and forgiven girls the girls the girls there are always more – girls who should begin to sing, who should ask sincerely and raise a hand if they feel, who sit at the end in tight circles of girls and bring their shaky eyelids down and the first prayer a tarantula

scraggles out of my mouth

2.
___

Vocab

learning
to say this,
gradually: *disturbance   white smoke*
honey   silence
holding the horses back,
holding them
back from the mind with
little, citrus   contact   translation
a book with two columns on every page
so how do you say: *I prayed*
in a snowstorm   into my fist   against
myself   began to spill out
I write a prayer down in this language
copy it out again in the other
practise stroke order
write each verb
in its dictionary form:
to beg   to change   to witness

After such a fall as this

Through the slick
lonely automatic doors
I run in a moment
and never consider
how much of this
is a part of me,
the green wallpaper
the lumpy walls of
my throat, this
creak of a chair
a knot for my shoulder,
and jars of pickled plums
sealed too tight
are there to be
smashed to find
no easy, dismissible
snack but something
like, something like
this, a pulp and it
tastes like I push
on the next
revolving door
swivelling into a
mostly empty very
scrubbed how all
the best institutes
start my guide laughs
leading me by the waist
here where I strain
at the heavy oak
door and how could
I not go in, the others
are now so far away
with their cold
crunchy politics,
this hubbub anyway
so scuffed and fizzy
takes me just as I am,
there's hardly enough
of me left near
the centre of the earth,
garden gate, dogs

in the fragile lake, I'm
punching the code
for the door I always
knew as this singing
whirs behind my
teeth and I can't
see what's next but
I do what they
tell me, and never
once think of
how to get back.

Wherever the body is

My soul doth magnify the Lord
who melts the snow in grubby, chunky heaps.
As stretches of honest pavement reappear it gets safer

to shed jumpers, take deeper breaths,
wake up at sunrise and fold the futon,
and go to church. I want to run –

I want to run to run to what,
for what? Is this a phase –
For he hath regarded the lowliness of his handmaiden

who folds a page of her new NIV
in the karaoke room, mid-afternoon,
and clicks open her pen.

The reason the world does not know us –
it did not know him. What would I ask him?
In the spangly tenth-floor cabin I scribble,

A handful of beautiful, freshly cut jewels,
Continually cleansed until we get to heaven,
I don't want, I can't let this be just a phase.

Wherever the body is
(new patches of grass, corn stalls, businessmen
hack into cobs

as we open the doors, set up the chairs,
position the lights) there the eagles
will be gathered together.

Friday night – pizza party.
Hi I'm from London, yes London, a meaningless sound.
Create in me a clean heart, O my rope.

Every good gift

Susukino at dusk is a place superimposed on a place – behind the crackling abundance of stacked moisturiser and bundles of stockings the mountains jostle together in permanent blue, rubbed and buffed by the clean north winds of Hokkaido.

Scripture burns my mouth like a cob of corn hotter and oilier than expected, wrapped in plastic that drips its salty sauce – I walk a few blocks and wait for it to cool, hold it outstretched like a goldfish won at the fair.

Hot canned coffee outside the building as people scuffle past out of our lives and they go unprotected away from us. Should a prayer feel sloppy and wet in the praying? Should it feel like this, as they walk away some jittery, timid words against hell, though she cups the coffee can, slowly repeats *Hell is not knowing you're already there.*

I'm small, made of something like watery rice milk, held by a parent figure though this is more fabric than clear memory, the smell of plucked wet leaves, the weakness, can't lift my arms over my head. I saw her call him Papa in her notebook this morning – so I try it too, Papa Papa – ask him to carry me over the junction.

Saviour anxiety

Twenty new specimens
wings taped down
labelled *healer, producer,*
noisemaker, beak-
snap and snapped
mucky but clear-eyed, that's
how he wanted us,
fans out our wings
on cotton,
bone pinned down,
slips back out for the rest but dawn's
spilling out soon all silence
or squawk –
the rest of them hop
from foot to foot not so
easy to catch
they sniff
the air –
the flakes of him
left on bark –
the trees he brushed
against to get to them –
his ankles
so easy to peck
and fray – his lips
so good to snatch for a nest,
for a hole but not if he gets there first –
one on the left side one on the right
and three more: the bitter
muscular ones,
he bathes them in liquid,
writes comments on stomachs and beaks
or question marks
or a dash
and he presses everyone flat
on the sheets, only my legs jerk up
and his wrist jogs
I settle into this what
do I want do I
want this
he labels each one
of us *What   can   I   make*
them   do   all   day.

Iron & Iron

Friend sharpens friend –
We ring against
each other – We polish
each other's commitment –
Our stories clang
together – We craft testimony –
At last I found joy,
a weighty metal –
We snap
the communion cracker
in a crisp sun – It feels
protective – On clean
lined pages we copy
the words that shimmer
like mirrors – To love as loved –
To cut through different
qualities of thought – To be
a strong blade – I turn
persuasive –
I put a cold hand to my chest
where we learn the death is –
Here – It's heavy and hot –
I mirror the words
exactly – I tell my new friend
In our polished bodies
we carry a death and it glints
in our chests – It welds
us together –

Fervent Book

Effective, fervent prayer becomes a goal, to hack and pick at communication –
write it in red, until it feels true:
a fervent prayer *will* have an effect, the 'effective' prayer has got to be fervent.

*

from the fruit of our lips / we're filled with goodness

*

To put God ahead of flipflopping emotion. To put you. Write it again.
To put you you you – to pin myself to you like a moth. Praise as a form of understanding
The ramen ads get greener, greener
Proverbs 4. Psalm 62. Ezekiel 8 –

With an urgent underscoring piano Son of man would you look north – dig into the wall, behind the door these paintings of crawling things, unclean freaks, seventy elders in green glass spluttering a sick belief that nothing matters while every creak of your joints, your thoughts is being witnessed, Son of man.

*

Open a little book on the ninth floor, matcha latte, *but let patience have its perfect work*

Open the book in Mos Burger, *that you may be perfect and complete, lacking nothing*

Open the book in the udon shop, an anxious, noodly feeling, guarding against (unspecified) sin

*

And what hurts? Did snow hurt, and will it hurt again? Does my skin hurt, cracking and red at dawn, two claws clawing my way out of the futon? Do ankles hurt? Does my ineffectiveness hurt, or my uselessness, a flabby pale face in the underground tunnel, on the slow escalator? Does the journal, do the corners of a bible, does an email? Does it hurt to write an explanation, or delete it? Do my knees underneath the heated coffee table on the highest most brutal setting get burnt, and hurt? Does the Japanese language hurt, sitting in my windpipe like pickled fruit?

*

he gives strength to the weary / they will walk and not be faint

*

so here I am trying it, God, God like a clean red cut from the sea
On a still and windless night
& if love is not just emotional but a response to a commandment
Please watch your step. Please watch your step

In the evening, the city will cool and harden;
I'll walk towards them all in the dark.

*

fix your gaze directly before you

*

the piano
starts a clear clear
image a man like crystal
an underground river with bare
collarbones slow chords a feeling like
just before a scream a rush of breath we
open our eyes and sit down you're
heavy and bright this glowing
in my stomach eternal as
eternal as I need
you to be

*

would all of you throw me down / this leaning wall / this tottering fence

3.

Immorality

i.

Our plane falls towards a stretch of river dark as charcoal and very still we nosedive down it's disappointing I wake up.

Sudden godlessness in the dark a screeching sound a plane overhead.

A small stone turtle swims against a current of grey pebbles towards a slab of rock.

An open space of pebbles is raked and raked by monks, the eternal sea they're never allowed to forget, and the glossy bamboo feels like madness and plastic.

Blindfolded high school kids fumble their way from one lucky stone to the other and here's my translated fortune, *You will misunderstand each other.*

What happens if I crack *hard* the spine of my bible *ha,* like *this* and snapping the pages scream with anger searching for an appropriate verse, Be sober-minded; be watchful.

During last night's deep-fried everything on sticks I numbed my mouth with heat and oil and finally read –

Octopus, eel, green pepper, pumpkin, remember, lotus root, remember, battered and, battered and, decisions take time but the rules write battered and skewered forms of sin the ways

and ways to think and live in chewy gold, with an oily gold crust, and do I accept with a godly gold crust can I gulp that, will I gulp it, gulp it down.

I wake up godless, or I wake up and experiment with waking up godless, or waking up thinking *I'm godless* which would mean the same thing, if I actually thought it.

Bare-shouldered on the balcony with pencil-coloured light and godlessness like suddenly taking off headphones – silence.

How we came to the thatched yellow house at the edge of the yellow field and stepped inside gently, a tidy poem.

These decisions take time she says in the doorway rubbing at my arm beginning to wrap my neck in gold string winding it down and down my torso it's inescapable I wake up.

ii.
Psalmwork is
violent and gives
no answers:
mountains slide
slide slide into
the sea and
a whirling boy
is David floodlit
chewing his
hands attempting
attempting
to speak to you,
to ask for enemies
shredded and
pulped though
still he names
you fortress,
refuge as if for
the likes of us
at least you're
safe – September
air humid like
sponge cake in
a dark café
pulling pieces
off a sponge cake,
I try to reconcile
shepherd/warrior
and *He is our*
fortress they
loudly insist, let
me open their
heads I'd see
their neon
glittering
certain brains
but you are not
safe, not a soft
shape – you
unfold in me
your allergens,
a waxy bud to
the lip then the
gum the gut
the spikes of

the grass the
wings of a wasp
as sheets of
rainwater spill
down *September*
September September,
punishment, a
divisive light
you are,
punishment,
you freeze/
pixellate my
faraway boyfriend
How would I
rate the quality
of my call Our
father father father
slaughters
particular sheep,
I roll that
around on
my swollen
tongue, sleeping
a hard thick
heavy block
of a sleep will
not fix this. As
the deer pants
for streams
of water, what
I don't know
can't also be
knowledge,
what's
unacceptable
is not faith, a
collapsing pile
of shells, the
dependable
shells shells shells
make me sick
like communion,
like certainty
how dare you
assume, how
dare you

dictate but
still every
Sunday I
nearly break
into a run on
the way to
you so what
is a boyfriend,
a homeland
when the park
is full of rice-
stuffed squid,
sea urchins
are black shiny
beasts slit down
the middle and
just a glimpse,
a flicker of
their gooey
yellow – as the
deer drinks
the difficult
water so I keep
reading on
thin paper
that the kindness
you practice is
boundaried,
and when
unbelievers
leave, you
let them.

iii.

Devotion pares me down –
northern sea, fresh fish, knife to cut a question out.

As snowflies push the air I stop rustling
and kicking and fall still – there is a universe

in which a problem exists and another in which
you push again against

all pristine logic, I pick you up
and your neck clicks back, your head

falls back, the battery in your chest crackles
stand up – leave your mother father lover –

pack your precious self into a cube for me –
you crackle *peace, peace*

I leave with you – a dripping circle
hovering here in the part of my brain

where I only want, where I pick
a universe. Press myself to it. Each line of prayer

becomes hot, unbreakable,
Your eyes to my eyes Your skin to my skin –

in this heat we worshippers starfish our hands
or clutch ourselves as if stabbed or as if

it's the first time we've ever worshipped
and we've known nothing, nothing like it and yes,

I fall in with this code –
by loosening the body I become pliable,

a loosened body is trusting, you stream down
my throat like cold apple juice and my fists

open out, outside it turns colder,
the city is softly frosted Lego,

mountains surround the city
expecting everything.

Kiviaq

You die, so we make a bag of your skin
and pack you tight with sea birds.
You were our fruit-eyed neighbour, our charm,
loved and sketched by our daughters so now
we kiss your leathery cheek,
we dig you a pit.
And there you meet him, we know it,
and nibble his whiskers, lick his nose,
ask *Why do I heave with beak and feather*
cry out *Why pressing me down down deep*
but you squeak and swallow dirt.
Just wait.
Let the birds ferment.
They smell like the sea and the island's tip,
their wings twitch
and soften – their spike-feet soften – their beaks curl –
their eyes are unglued and open –
they gulp big bird-breaths in you
and grow lamp-hot
until the time of shovels,
no longer mammal or friend
but a pickle jar hauled out, uncorked
and a flow of birds for our land
and the daughters and rocks of our life,
your mercy, your meat.

Aurora Town

Listen   Listen   Listen to me   Let me tell you
what I've learned so far   Among sesame powders,
scallops on sticks a single cut of horse sashimi
is red and costly like a small tongue   A woman
sits across from me and says by thirteen she was
speaking in tongues   She tells me it feels like
bubbling water   She asks would I like to come
with them past bubbling stews   Gaijin bars
RAMEN-CHOCO   Boiled meats on a stick   In your
grid-town we know something good will happen
If we knock   If we listen   Each street a photo,
a bounce to our gestures   The covered walkway
theme tune on a loop   *Sap   Po   Ro*   In primary
colours   Shivery host boys   High school girls with
graduation flowers   Hitched-up skirts   And how
can they believe if they have not heard and how
can they hear without someone preaching and
how can anyone preach unless they are sent
so I head to the underground shopping streets
or into Starbucks   Tully's   Doutor   La Pausa
McDonald's   Vie de France   Outside the shrine
the dolphin balloons rustle together   Her flip
phone weighed down by toys   I let down the nets
for a catch   Listen   I am the clay, you are the potter
I've learned to feel so strongly for you and to say it
My brain echoes constantly   Thank you thank you
C'mon   C'mon   Can you hear it   She's looking
interested and I say with my newly sweetened
smile   See you Sunday   It feels so good   This
Food Brings Us A Wonderful Time   Matcha
drinks in trembling shades of green with green
ice cream and the girls eat foot-high green
parfaits with dinky spoons   And you tell me
when the storm has swept by the wicked are
gone and I believe you   Junior high school
baseball teams break and shift the old snow
with shovels   The righteous stand firm forever
The spring sun finally bursts, a piñata   Crucible
for silver and furnace for gold   Everything is
personal   Frisbee by the TV Tower   Jingles
Percussion   Vitamin Lemon   NIPPON-HAM

FIGHTERS Butter Roll I'm flammable, I'm
getting it right I know that this is what
you want Polaroids Fountains Revelations
Shaved ice Can you hear me Can you

Jupiter

we gather, lungs
hot and gritty
from singing,
my every word
until now was
a croak, planted
in sharp addictive
community all
this time a storm
was swirling,
on one parched
planet a red swell
and kneeling
into it love turns
counter-clockwise
in phosphorus,
ancient loneliness,
sensation of sound
before sound
is made, speak, I
always knew it
was there, speak,
scraping mud out
of a throat,
speak –
you pour out,
a colour
thrown by tongues

Dream after baptism

Terracotta bath into which I step.
What colour is the room – dim yellow.
The room is very hot (candlelit?). Oval
of water swirling with sparks
off the rim to be electric around me,
prepare me –
Tight red loop of muscle stretched out
holding the dream together.
Wouldn't she like to get married?
What does this mean to her?
To know your morning sun – Bathtub
cold as a pond in hungry greens –
spinning silvers – streaks of
conviction red
with a chime This is possible, possible
shining ever brighter till the full light of day
The path of the righteous.
And then in the name of,
Hold me right down for a long time
longer than the first time, bubbles stream
from me, I dig my nails
into the fish and claw them open.
I crackle all the way through.
No breath now, only a purging.

Book of Metals

As summer intensifies, a road trip – a southern village nicknamed Hell. Smoking craters, sulphurous baths, blue and red devils made of stone, signs explaining the forest's unholy insects. We giggle at the edge of the valley, a rusty bench, a position of assumed safety.

*

weeks become richer
huddled together
nowhere that's mine
mad about the boy

*

We sit under the trees behind the yakitori stall, and I speak in my recent, coppery voice.

And I touch my lips at odd moments, as if to trap this way of speaking, or uncertain how these words are coming from me.

I read out this verse from my phone, about *whatever we do in word or deed.*

*

Scrawling choice silver on pieces of paper:
worthy treasures, timely crops, the LORD said to me, a crown of blessings, accepting commands, walking in integrity, discipline, stepping stones, prudent, diligence, he who gathers crops in summer, my mouth a fountain of life

*

She hugs me goodbye and gets on the plane

On the TV a man bites into an apricot like it's his first

Midnight, hot pavement, cradled by air

*

& burning on the road can't hold this back could just
rise up *in psalms & hymns & spiritual songs* the sky is a fatherly blue

burning despite/because   & I love that I can just write it
like this   I, I, I   sing your name   Jesus, I
breathe it   I write it down
all over the page –

*

a koi in the pond
is there and not there
a slippery trick
in a clear habitat
a country I can only look at

4.

And whatever you do

Plucked
from the
middle of
the sun into
flurried airport
romaji I mean
Roman
alphabet *Heath –*
Row – Heath – Row –
here I
am, I think, a
keen and
purposeful
messenger
with so much
to give, so
much *fluent*
certainty
finally, properly
at my disposal
and this is
how the barriers
open, and
certainty starts
to ruin you.

Evangelism

On Paradise Row, I'm spillable –

leaves hurry down their promises, splatter the pavement red.

The season is reddish metal, hot scrubbed skin, sparks around me

testing my faith's qualities –

how deep it is, how bloodlike, how it clamours

like the red root tunnels twitching Bethnal, Bethnal underneath us.

Everyone should feel like this, lips licked over and over with purpose.

A pink scarf is meaningful in the wind.

If I threw a ball the sky would bruise.

Nobody sees me collect in a pool at your feet.

She's so

Tonguetied   Tonguerubbed   Tonguesmothered   Tonguesnagged   Tonguenoodled   Tonguejuiced   Tonguespun   Tonguebroken in a bus swerving off to the canal   Tonguecanaled and counting the men who are a useless unshuffled pack   Tongueyanked   Tonguetorn   Tonguegrilled   Tonguebashed a little runt too slow   a twitch a bish a bosh from palm to palm   Tonguesmoked   Tonguestunned by   (never had) a loud tongue like theirs   Tonguestunted forever by Chelsea and Knightsbridge   Tonguepurpled   Tonguestained   Tonguecracked and buckling at nonsense gardeners/   nannies/piano teachers/play therapists   Tonguebloodied double-decker bright   and clanking   Tonguecathedraled   Tonguewestended   Tongueredvelvetcaked   Tongueflipped inside out trying to make it *and very good at lying*

53

Prime Minister Material

Gone are the days we were compelling, now we are only casual.

He is a chewy, chickeny dumpling but not prime minister material.

Autumn gives rich, swollen eyes

to Holy Innocents, I think

but sometimes coffee just goes wrong

spikes my sadness

unplugs my modem

dents

my soup-can face.

Gone is the season our leader was sweet.

We watch him rummage the rulebook,

drink cool highland water,

go for jogs.

Our conferences always smell so crisp.

Our buffet breakfasts are endless, deserved.

Hey everyone it's me it's me, I'm on live TV trying to cross my legs

or clap like a nice guy or eat.

No. Like this.

We fall into armchairs. We sink into armchairs.

We kiss our partners,

our eyes dying phones.

Our lips a flicker of zingy post-its.

Surely we had something big to do what was it.

This morning I battered a spider hard hard hard with my leather boot.

Gone are the days we started well.

10 worship songs

watery Sunday
excuses
watery prayers of apology

oceans like wirewool
like quickly chopped salad
the physicality

how he spat on people
how he ate and talked about eating
stories of hunger and thirst

a bus another
another bus
crammed with sugary lambs like me

oh god I just listened
to that song again barley grains
stuck in my nails

to think *I'm praying* isn't praying
barbecue weather
the bread of

he asks me who do you say I am
who do you need me to be
I ask him that

tangled cross necklace
a nice tangly spangly vomity
I didn't mean this. I'm sorry

when we come to the edge
of the territory a kind of great
insect rubbing its legs all over me

and if your eye causes you
to stumble gouge it out
thanks for another day

Shabu-shabu

At the bowl of hot water, we slice our love thin.

Everyone we met we cut to pale, uncooked anecdotes –
at the table of musical meats we kneel, our meal waits

to be dipped, to hiss. We won't mourn one strip, just poach,
quick, eat – or let it drop, curl and shake and boil,

over-boil in the vat. Wherever we go we forget where we've been,
what we ate, how we cared. But you ribbon of beef – you hop,

splutter, beg for a rapture, sing out *ssshabu-shabu* just to be plucked
from the plentiful bath to our dipping sauce, to splash about

in sweet salt death, to be draped – righteous, cooked –
on warm white rice, gasping *Master gobble me, I hurl my flesh-love*

on your flesh – simply because you sizzled, writhed, coloured
beneath me, for a few seconds.

A great girl like you

Who am I to think like this   Do the bathrooms of all important people get
bigger and warmer, like this   Will the walls expand and sweat   If my friends
shrink to digital popcorn could I pluck   and eat them   My kitten
abandoned, outlawed   Was the city only ever this scummy green pool
I think to find my way into that   lovely garden which is always there, but
the city's longest/shortest escalators buzz and clunk   The garden waits in the north
of my map and no amount of   Evening Standards   clogging up the barriers could
ever tell me otherwise   If they make the tunnels at King's Cross so long
and bloodless on purpose   let them, let them   But I used to know this better
They said What do you want   Inhaler   Ribena   Do you pay for your
prescriptions   Have you used this before   This is to lift and stretch
your knotty limbs and toss   them up like a kite   and this is to pull
the limbs back down   and this is for when you are water   when you roil
and pulse like a world-famous river   and this is for when you are flat and stamped
as a tunnel   But if I could only have my pet   If I could kiss her scratchy fur and
carry her   over Battersea Bridge   But I used to know so many things
and I had my tiny, lovable hands   my monstrous hateful hands

God so loved the girl

I step inside the Corinthian room

which is full of young people freshly planted, brilliant white walls, shaking windows and look how the sun floods in and I flood a notebook hungrily, *For God so loved the world that he filled us all with a rich gold light* and how quickened we are, and will feast forever – how I've missed this feeling, cool fingers pressed to my burnt face, is this the home finally, our bodies becoming one gleaming, praising body with all the difficulty just sliced away and I'm free to copy this down, *The unleavened bread of sincerity – we must keep (scoured, unharmed, sequestered), Put out of your fellowship, Do not even eat with her, just a little patch is enough to Contaminate* For God so loved the world he split us into crap little boxes but I don't write this down, the thought just appears the instant I'm told not to think So loved the world he kicked it to death, So loved it he ripped it into chunks – how I take a very deep breath in and out, find myself sketching the dream where I'm hairy and much too big for the room, armpit hair clumps together, an unacceptable smell coming off me, the sketch collapses into these scribbly lines, this hunched heap of spikes outside a thick-edged square – how we bleed into 1 Samuel's manic king clutching his head spitting and gulping getting it so spectacularly wrong – scrabbling at the hem of a luckier, better, luckier man's robes – how we nod and praise this, *Desperate & Sad & Unforgiving* I scrawl without stopping, *So loved us he gave a fucked-up boy* how the silk of this falls away from thought to thought stabbing and inking a wobbly creature who never looked at me – did you ever look at me – did anything ever – For God so loved the girl he drained all the love back out of her, the glug of an emptying sink

and I leave the room

Click 'accept'

There was a way of living

scaly eczema fear peeled clean

cracked, small, ugly, raised
for crows to munch to nothing

drag a sack of angry thoughts

deliberate idiocy

her words a sunflower
by wanting faith we gain it.

by not wanting

apologise to the thin air
never ever ever

we lose it

This game is called *Animals*

Kleinsong

the discovery of hate
makes   me   feel   like   a
block of wood   presses me down
to a scrawny spitmouth can't believe
the milk of you, as revelations
drop like heavy coins *mucky*
mother makes a girl but remember
when oil was separate from water,
I liked, liked it better, felt like
the maker, when I wanted the good
moon came and the bad moon rotted
and sank when I wanted, reliable
sky full of nothing but milk and never
before to contend with this Dis-
appointment/knocking
inside me/the good moon's
smirk the bad moon's pool/
a knocking to bite to spoil this
puckering cream of the sky because
actually you're a muddied one
guiltily bitten, aren't, aren't you
in   cinema   orchestra   can't stop
you slide into every persons fill out
their faces with cruelty and milk,
was I ever your daughter crammed
as you are with toothy wrigglesome
baby baby sisters how can I stand
it how   can   I   go   on   without
this to wrap my teething self
around, must've hacked you good/
bad in half and now what can I
holding the pieces together what
can I kill off a sullied parent
what can I hurt with
these hard gums

Congruence

It's like It's like this Like a girl who won't Like a girl
pressing buttons on/off with her elbow Not able

to type To wash To pick up those dropped frozen
peaches Like this I could say I could search for it

At Finchley Rd she's a crumbly wafer and can't admit
Though they all want to hear Though only if useful

Though wrists smeared with ink are ugly, unsafe
She clicks in the cold But I don't know how else

It's like Bellowing Bellowing worship songs over
the mouldy sink again or writing *not going to write*

in here for a while None of this is defence or release
With Finchley Road's bully arrhythmia telling me

Myth has some very cruel baggage Observing
You were just lonely that's all Yanking up the sour facts

These petulant nerve endings ready to snap
You come across as anxious and it's a real shame

I dream my old leader orchestrating a group hug
Group hug everyone she says But I have this This

osteopetrosis Or arms stuck straight out and any
moment limbs could cringe and slip *Look at you*

she chimes *What's the matter* Their voices ring
in the air and chime They chime the story better

than me And meanwhile the rainbow above us
so heavy, swollen and juicy Will it Will it burst

Can I push the North Circular slowly down my throat
like a grey ribbon I think that would make this OK,

would make Brent Cross bearable Can I smother
all this Can I chop up this feeling like a block

of butter Can I chop it into cubes and melt the cubes
into a stew she would scoop up with a spoon and say

I think you have some things to process It's a shame
Can I chop this feeling like a bad onion

It's like It's just like To be congruent with you
would be like gradually turning warmer saying

Look at all these rituals Aren't we childlike My red
fingertips Nothing in my gut but warmth and a little

acidic sloshing You all come into focus Let me be useful
Can I contribute Something I promise you Something

happened Now stay with this feeling What's it trying
to say What does it need Contain us forever

Little birds and beasts

I functioned in my obvious world
I sat on the train with Tesco sushi, sucking ginger straight from the pouch
I watched the train weave through luxury developments
I learned an unblinking spite
I learned *You should astonish, constantly*
I saw a bread roll dropped and frightened on Kingsway
My vision whirled
I had haircuts
I had several good jobs one after the other
I sat on the F R A G I L E R O O F
I made eye contact with vulnerable people
I tripped over on Fleet Street
I continued to schedule meetings and type *Kind regards*
The stars popped and rolled above me
I bought heel grips
I found a cube of air next to a luxury development
I swayed inside it
I couldn't count higher than such-and-such a number
I thought the contents of the sink were trying to shout but I didn't say so
I believed no one
I sat in the bar with a nasty drink
We fell in love
I buckled
I heard him referred to as a *lovely lovely man*
My dress was very purple
I got the keys to the castle
I got a box of vitamin shakes
I was referred to as *exquisite – however…*
I saw the white arrows all over the road and followed them
I continued to sculpt my inadequate hair
I learned that actually 98% of every espresso is water
The bus jumped up and my head jerked forward
I couldn't stop
I was not influential
I tripped over, not famously
When the little birds and beasts tapped *HOW STUPID* to each other I said
"How stupid!"
I went to an expensive clinic
I enjoyed blame of all kinds
I went to Malta
I grabbed my hair and pulled
My internal judge said this and that
One morning I met this absolute bitch

'Wild Talents'

after Susan Hiller

Holy Ghost, you are not so nice.
Deep welts you have opened across my back.
I press against the wall in case you sneak up.
The clicking slides are surely yours.
In the spoon that scraped along the ledge, in the girl's shuffling cup of syrup
You insist you were not but I know better.
They say every house had its goblin once, they've credited such papery imps.
Candle after candle, no one but you.
In Morse code, every time.
You made the girl rise like a dandelion seed.
You were felt moving in the floor at Nicaea.
You licked poor Simeon's ear and convinced him of you.
You took them all in your blinding, enormous palm as if they were marbles
And there they are jangling.
But I am not so forgiving.
The clicking – your skewered and panicked locust.
The girl jumped up – she tore the clicking contraption from her head,
She would not move toy trains with her mind, not ever again.
'When we were young we believed Fantastic Things'
And you promised such wild talents but you didn't ever lift or place me,
Nor ready my voice into that sick whoop.
I can walk out of this room cool and steady.
I can sit in another town, winter solstice or no –
And if the alarm goes off, if the cards spill from the table, if you gather again
At my trembling sliding eyes I will not flinch

5.

Cathedral

We were certain of our needs. We divided the landscape: some buildings were *harmonious,* others were *trash.* We wanted the skyline to chime. We'd feel calmer soon. The city's structures muttered, like a choir tuning up.

This particular heap we had gutted completely, but its gold exterior dazzled us. What was it? What had it ever produced? Its domes flashed carelessly, sloppily, reflected in the river.

In its place, we wanted something eternal – a mass of strong new materials. A statue would crown the structure, hollowed out so we could move around inside him. There would be a library in his forehead, a social club in his outstretched arm.

On the day of demolition I was bedridden, all the compartments of my mind echoing as if struck one by one with a stick. Can you imagine – the smashing together of wax and gold, ceiling and infant, wine and floor?

Did we look out in any direction, a yellow rose, a red badge, all the words we'd never need, swallowing hard the rugs, the scarves

I half-remember these blueprints of us. How
the older technologies buckled
on us. How

I stepped into a

famous new swimming pool,

and began to do these laps

Cold Black Tea

I carry the baby over the junction
away from the rooms of all my friends
up to the gate of the darkening chapel
I carry her in a peach leather handbag
filled with cold, black tea
she bobs up and down hairless and faceless
sloshes around sloshes around
pale and soft as a freshly peeled egg
an ethanol tang in the air
nail polish remover
mothers
coins
over the junction away from these people
who want to ask questions
who won't go away
a blanket over my floating baby
we reach the door and they come so close
excuse me, hello, excuse me please
how do we get to the festival
where are your trampled grandmothers
all those resilient women
I look and my baby is not in the bag which is dripping
I'll never remain intact
where is the snow
and tell us who was it
who stood up and left the room
declaring they couldn't help you with this

Sunflower

Cool white stone. Thick cool white walls. Pearls
stitched in loops, waves, round the gaps where

saints could be, but Anna, Mikhail, red wing chipped
(flaked) away to blank stone

Pink, Teal, Gold

Pigeons (pigeons), sunflower seeds.
Baking white brick, bits of broken-up road.
Humidity – intensifier.
Rucksack filled with boiling Pepsi.
One version of tourism chokes the gold room,
sensational stories are told in a language the monks can't correct
(birds swoop in and out).
Lose crumbs of grammar the whole structure fails.
Marrow and thyme, blue effortful stars.
The same image from a raised platform
(martyrs, their faces peeling, taped-up) –

Pigeons (devotion), sunflower seeds.
Baking white brick (bubbling white brickwork).
Bits of broken-up bits of road.
Rucksack filled with boiling poems
crumbs of grammar marrow and thyme
(a structure of blue, focused stars).
Sensational stories the monks don't correct,
humidity, the golden room.
Birds swoop in (Pepsi-Cola).
The image from this platform, this one.
Old, repairable martyrs

20 *worship songs*

a shiny patch, burnt. to hold a thumb up
or a temple, a shoulder blade, this is where
it happened, I could say, look, I let it in.

where smoke was created, a butterfly
fell on a wire, a red star folded in on
itself – with a crackling, inevitable sound.

A five-minute walk
happened in my mind. I unpeeled it from
the back of my brain. A three-year walk happened.

if I wriggle a thumb through the hole of
this fabric what else will bite what else
can I will back into existence –

remember the very first relief
of it so simple it
couldn't've been real

Aurora Town, texting
a psalm that begged
for cleansing too much

She was tangled in bibles and journal papers,
cross-legged on a blow-up bed hunched
over talking into a laptop –

the pose of transition –
using urgent, clipped words as if she hadn't just typed
I can barely cross the apartment, let alone the world

a rawness, a paleness
onions and pink sliced meat
like dipping the meat in gold raw egg was confusing

things pushed
into spaces they weren't
supposed to

She kept trying to end this, not
a girl in slacks staggering forward the path
behind her crumbling etc,

Not friends who step back and become just people
a silvery film all over their faces
closed bank accounts, wavy mountains in summer

not a person who leaves the stage
mid-scene, not prayers
with the wrong words in

I broke crackers into bits
poured tea into tiny cups
crunched and drank you up

Laugh, laugh, laugh
Somebody wrote:
Or I wrote:

There was goodness, remembered in a kind of
untouchable way, the same way you'd respond to
a strange animal sitting in your lap. What do I do with this

I lift each sentence out
like an old gown –
what to do with it?

Can I sweep my arms
across it all as if
across a desk –

or stitch toothy pearl sentences
around the space where
hunger's always been

where a room
will always
hold itself, ready.

The Lizard

The men talk, the men were raised to talk, the men are assured as they gesture and talk at England's most southerly point.

They've climbed to the edge of their own dark rocks at the country's end to pick apart a world through a gate swung boldly open for debate, chewing, policy, horizon physics, irrational sainthood, chapters of knottiest Cornish writings where *the end of the land is imminent…*

where I want to speak too, with an accuracy – in *balsamic* land, that old *speaking* ache… and though the churning green in front of us could kill us it feels secular, we can talk it out, unpick, unpick it.

But my not-guilty creative voice, my creative guilty not-voice, my guilty voice, not creative, not ever at the root, is a voice held in a sack, *disgrace*, a flinty hot mind attacking itself

as this man says the book's most compelling ideas are the high priest's roomy questions and doubts, his comfort in these rooms of doubt which echo *let's, let's consider, consider, consider, consider*

In slipped sun, light as harsh as rock, the gate bangs shut, the boys continue urgently talking, wild ponies get right into the grass and mud to slop away at some chewable grace, I steady myself
a version of myself to say that doubt is sleet emerging cutting sideways

against a small hunched figure who tried to hack a path, equated doubt with loss and lost, climbed to the edge of a story to tell – to try – to never – a witness at the end of the land always about to get right in and say it.

And there was morning

She was never delicate – no dish of sugar –
but what does she need to love to feel stronger?
The knife pierced a lung.

The first chapter's damaged emerald leaves
And there was evening, and there was
As she staggered away she felt something beginning.

When the clouds part, is she being considered –
the way she might peel off a scrap of her lip,
balance it on her finger?

Acknowledgements

Thank you to the editors of the following publications in which early versions of some of these poems have appeared: *3:AM, Ambit, Blue of Noon, B O D Y, The Bohemyth, The Literateur, Magma, Queen Mob's Tea House, Poems In Which, Poetry London, Poetry Wales, Powder Keg.*

'Pods' borrows lines from 'My Heart Will Go On' by Celine Dion, 'Total Eclipse of the Heart' by Bonnie Tyler, 'God Only Knows' by the Beach Boys and 'Wuthering Heights' by Kate Bush. Thanks and apologies to anyone who's ever done karaoke with me.

The last line of 'Click 'accept'' is taken from *Put Your Mother on the Ceiling* by Richard De Mille, as quoted in *Windows to our Children* by Violet Oaklander.

'The Lizard' borrows some images and misremembered phrases from *The Living Stones: Cornwall* by Ithell Colquhoun.

The titles of and some phrases from 'After such a fall as this', 'A great girl like you' and 'Little birds and beasts' are taken from *Alice's Adventures in Wonderland* by Lewis Carroll.

The biblical phrases and materials in some of the poems have been borrowed from the New International Version, the King James Bible, the New King James Version, the New Living Translation and the English Standard Version. The text used in 'Wherever the body is' is taken from the Magnificat.

Huge thanks to Broken Sleep, and to Aaron for being so great to work with.

Thank you to everyone who at various points encouraged me to keep writing this – Adham, Charly, Tom, Richard, Imogen, Dom and Team Tera. Thanks always to Mum, Dad, Misha and my family in Moscow and Sydney.

Thanks especially to Tom, for everything.

LAY OUT YOUR UNREST

9 781913 642754